ISBN 978-1-5283-2606-3
PIBN 10899212

A Briefe and True Relation of the Discouerie of the North Part of

VIRGINIA

By JOHN BRERETON

Reproduced in *Facsimile* from the First Edition of 1602

With an Introductory Note by

LUTHER S. LIVINGSTON

NEW YORK
DODD, MEAD & COMPANY
1903

Introductory Note

THE little book reproduced on the succeeding pages is the account, by one of the men of the expedition, of the first voyage of Englishmen to the shores of New England. Captain Gosnold and thirty-two others set sail from Falmouth on Friday, March 26, 1602, and made their first landing on Cape Cod, which they so named on account of the great abundance of fish found there. This was the first English name given to any part of the New England coast. They also discovered and named the Island of Martha's Vineyard. The small number in the party made the establishment of a colony impossible, and no extensive explorations were undertaken. They set out on their return on June 18, again on a Friday, and arrived safely in the harbor of Exmouth on July 23. This hasty voyage was the true beginning of New England.

Captain Gosnold was afterwards second in command in the little fleet which set sail for Virginia on December 20, 1606, under Captain Christopher Newport, and was a member of "His Majestie's Counsel of His First Colony in Virginia." He died there on August 22, 1607.

Brereton, the author of the narrative, may have held some minor office, at least he was one of the five men in the first boat which landed on Cape Cod. "Captain Bartholomew Gosnold, my selfe, and three others, went ashore," is the way he describes (on page 4) the landing of the first Englishmen on the shores of New England. Little or nothing is known of his after history, unless he be the same John Brereton who was convicted of manslaughter and pardoned in 1611, or the John Brereton who sought a license to keep an inn in Chester in 1613.

On page 14 is a little note of the fruitless voyage of Captain Samuel Mace, the same year, to Virginia by Raleigh's orders, to search for the lost colony at Roanoke. The "larger discourse" seems never to have "come to light," and but little is known of the voyage.

Captain Edward Hayes, the author of the "Treatise," described on the title, and which fills pages 15 to 24, was not, apparently, of the party, though he had himself been one of the pioneers in American colonization, having commanded the Golden Hinde, the companion to Sir Humphrey Gilbert's ill-fated ship, in the expedition to Newfoundland in 1583.

Two editions of the *Relation* were published in 1602. Of the first, which is the one reproduced, only three copies seem to be known. One was in the library of the late Lord Chancellor Hardwicke, being bound in with eleven other rare tracts, mostly relating to America. When his library was dispersed at Christie's in 1888, the volume brought £555. The Brereton from the collection is now in the John Carter-Brown Library in Providence. The second, from which our reproduction is made, belongs to Mr. E. D. Church, of New York. The third, which lacks title-page, is owned in England.

This first edition contains 24 pages only. The second has 48 pages and has the additional lines on the title-page: "With diuers instructions of speciall moment/ newly added in this second im-/pression." Of this second issue four copies can be traced in this country:

1. The fine Isham copy, entirely uncut, bought by Quaritch in the Isham sale in 1886 for £265. This afterwards belonged to the late Mr. Charles H. Kalbfleisch and to Mr. M. C. Lefferts. It now belongs to Mr. E. D. Church.

2. The Brinley copy, bought in that sale by Mr. Kalbfleisch, who, after the Isham sale, sold it to Messrs. Dodd,

Mead & Co., from whose hands it passed into Mr. Church's collection. Since Mr. Church has secured the Isham-Kalbfleisch-Lefferts copy, the Brinley-Kalbfleisch copy has in turn gone to Mr. E. E. Ayer, of Chicago.

3. The Barlow copy, which at that sale in 1890 brought $1,125 and is now in the New York Public Library, Lenox Collection.

4. A copy in the John Carter-Brown Library in Providence.

There are three copies of the second edition in the British Museum, one, in the Grenville collection, very imperfect.

L. S. L.

A
Briefe and true Relation of the Discouerie of the North part of *Virginia*; being a most pleasant, fruitfull and commodious soile:

Made this present yeere 1602, by Captaine *Bartholomew Gosnold*, Captaine *Bartholowmew Gilbert*, and diuers other gentlemen their associats, by the permission of the honourable knight, Sir WALTER RALEGH, &c.

Written by M. Iohn Brereton *one of the voyage.*

Whereunto is annexed a Treatise, conteining important inducements for the planting in those parts, and finding a passage that way to the South sea, and *China.*

Written by M. Edward Hayes, *a gentleman long since imploied in the like action.*

LONDINI,
Impensis Geor. Bishop.
1602.

To the honourable, Sir Walter Ralegh, *Knight, Captaine of her* Maiesties Guards, Lord Warden of the Stanneries, Lieutenant of *Cornwall*, and Gouernour of the Isle of *Iersey*.

Honourable sir, being earnestly requested by a deere friend, to put downe in writing, some true relation of our late performed voyage to the North parts of Virginia; at length I resolued to satisfie his request, who also imboldened me, to direct the same to your honourable consideration; to whom indeed of duetie it perteineth.

May it please your Lordship therefore to vnderstand, that vpon the sixe and twentieth of March 1602, being Friday, we went from Falmouth, being in all, two & thirtie persons, in a small barke of Dartmouth, called The Concord, holding a course for the North part of Virginia: and although by chance the winde fauoured vs not at first as we wished, but inforced vs so farre to the Southward, as we fell with S. Marie, one of the islands of the Açores (which was not much out of our way) yet holding our course directly from thence, we made our iourney shorter (than hitherto accustomed) by the better part of a thousand leagues, yet were we longer in our passage than we expected; which happened, for that our barke being weake, we were loth to presse her with much saile; also, our sailers being few, and they none of the best, we bare (except in faire weather) but low saile; besides, our going vpon an vnknowen coast, made vs not ouer-bolde to

They fel with S Marie, one of the Açores.

stand in with the shore, but in open weather; which caused vs to be certeine daies in sounding, before we discouered the coast, the weather being by chance, somewhat foggie. But on Friday the foureteenth of May, early in the morning, we made the land, being full of faire trees, the land somewhat low, certeine hummocks or hilles lying into the land, the shore ful of white sand, but very stony or rocky. And standing faire alongst by the shore, about twelue of the clocke the same day, we came to an anker, where sixe Indians, in a Baske-shallop with mast and saile, an iron grapple, and a kettle of copper, came boldly aboord vs, one of them apparelled with a wastcoat and breeches of blacke serdge, made after our sea-fashion, hose and shoes on his feet; all the rest (sauing one that had a paire of breeches of blue cloth) were all naked. These people are of tall stature, broad and grim visage, of a blacke swart complexion, their eie-browes painted white; their weapons are bowes and arrowes: it seemed by some words and signes they made, that some Basks or of S. Iohn de Luz, haue fished or traded in this place, being in the latitude of 43 degrees. But riding heere, in no very good harbour, and withall, doubting the weather, about three of the clocke the same day in the afternoone we weighed, & standing Southerly off into sea the rest of that day and the night following, with a fresh gale of winde, in the morning we found our selues embayed with a mightie headland; but comming to an anker about nine of the clocke the same day, within a league of the shore, we hoised out the one halfe of our shallop, and captaine Bartholmew Gosnold, my selfe, and three others, went ashore, being a white sandie and very bolde shore; and marching all that afternoon with our muskets on our necks, on the highest hilles which we saw (the weather very hot) at length we perceiued this headland to be parcell of the maine, and sundrie Islands lying almost round about it: so returning (towards euening) to our shallop (for by that time, the other part was brought ashore and set together) we espied an Indian, a yong man, of proper stature, and of a pleasing countenance; and after some familiaritie with him, we left him at the sea side, and returned to our ship, where, in fiue or sixe houres absence, we had pestered our ship so with Cod fish, that we threw numbers

They discouered land the 14. of May.

Sixe Indians come aboord of them.

The description of them.

Their first landing.

Another Indian.

An excellent Cod fishing.

bers of them ouer-boord againe: and surely, I am persuaded that in the moneths of March, April, and May, there is vpon this coast, better fishing, and in as great plentie, as in Newfound-land: for the sculles of Mackerell, herrings, Cod, and other fish, that we dayly saw as we went and came from the shore, were woonderfull; and besides, the places where we tooke these Cods (and might in a few daies haue laden our ship) were but in seuen faddome water, and within lesse than a league of the shore; where, in Newfound-land they fish in fortie or fiftie fadome water, and farre off. From this place, we sailed round about this headland, almost all the points of the compasse, the shore very bolde: but as no coast is free from dangers, so I am persuaded, this is as free as any; the land somwhat lowe, full of goodly woods, but in some places plaine: at length we were come amongst many faire Islands, which we had partly discerned at our first landing; all lying within a league or two one of another, and the outermost not aboue sixe or seuen leagues from the maine: but comming to an anker vnder one of the, which was about three or foure leagues from the maine, captaine Gosnold, my selfe, and some others, went ashore, & going round about it, we found it to be foure English miles in compasse, without house or inhabitant, sauing a little old house made of boughes, couered with barke, an olde piece of a weare of the Indians, to catch fish, and one or two places, where they had made fires. The chiefest trees of this Island, are Beeches and Cedars; the outward parts all ouergrowen with lowe bushie trees, three or foure foot in height, which beare some kinde of fruits, as appeared by their blossomes; Strawberies, red and white, as sweet and much bigger than ours in England, Rasberies, Gooseberies, Hurtleberies, and such; an incredible store of Vines, aswell in the woodie part of the Island, where they run vpon euery tree, as on the outward parts, that we could not goe for treading vpon them: also, many springs of excellent sweet water, and a great standing lake of fresh water, neere the sea side, an English mile in compasse, which is mainteined with the springs running exceeding pleasantly thorow the woodie grounds which are very rockie. Here are also in this Island, great store of Deere, which we saw, and other beasts, as appeared

A great headland.

Many faire Islands.

The first Island called Marthaes vineyard.

Beeches. Cedars.

Vines in abundance.

Springs. A Lake.

Deere. Other beasts.

Cranes. Hernshawes. Bitters. Geese. Mallards. Teales.

peared by their tracks; as also diuers fowles, as Cranes, Hernshawes, Bitters, Geese, Mallards, Teales, and other fowles, in great plenty; also, great store of Pease, which grow in certeine plots all the Island ouer. On the North side of this Island we found many huge bones and ribbes of Whales. This Island, as also all the rest of these Islands, are full of all sorts of stones fit for building; the sea sides all couered with stones, many of them glistering and shining like minerall stones, and very rockie: also, the rest of these Islands are replenished with these commodities, and vpon some of them, inhabitants; as vpon an Island to the Northward, and within two leagues of this; yet wee found no townes, nor many of their houses, although we saw manie Indians, which are tall big boned men, all naked, sauing they couer their priuy parts with a blacke tewed skin, much like a Black-smithes apron, tied about their middle and betweene their legs behinde: they gaue vs of their fish readie boiled (which they carried in a basket made of twigges, not unlike our osier) whereof we did eat, and iudged them to be fresh water fish: they gaue vs also of their Tabacco, which they drinke greene, but dried into powder, very strong and pleasant, and much better than any I haue tasted in England: the necks of their pipes are made of clay hard dried (whereof in that Island is great store both red and white) the other part, is a piece of hollow copper, very finely closed and semented together: we gaue vnto them certeine trifles, as kniues, points, and such like, which they much esteemed. From hence we went to another Island, to the Northwest of this, and within a league or two of the maine, which we found to be greater than before we imagined, being 16 English miles at the least in compasse; for it conteineth many pieces or necks of land, which differ nothing frō seuerall Islands, sauing that certeine banks of small bredth do like bridges ioyne them to this Island: on the outsides of this Island are many plaine places of grasse, abundance of Strawberies & other berries before mentioned: in mid May we did sowe in this Island (as for a triall) in sundry places, Wheat, Barley, Oats, and Pease, which in foureteene daies were sprung vp nine inches and more: the soile is fat and lustie; the vpper crust, of gray

Tabacco.

Elizabeths Island.

Wheat, Barley, and Oats sowed, came vp nine inches in foureteene dayes.

colour.

colour; but a foot or lesse in depth, of the colour of our hempe-lands in England; and being thus apt for these and the like graines; the sowing or setting (after the ground is cleansed) is no greater labour, than if you should set or sowe in one of our best prepared gardens in England. This Iland is full of high timberd Oaks, their leaues thrise so broad as ours; Cedars, strait and tall; Beech, Elme, Hollie, Walnut trees in abundance, the fruit as bigge as ours, as appeared by those we found vnder the trees, which had lien all the yeere vngathered; Hasenut trees, Cherry trees, the leafe, barke and bignesse not differing from ours in England, but the stalke beareth the blossomes or fruit at the end thereof, like a cluster of Grapes, forty or fifty in a bunch; Sassafras trees great plentie all the Iland ouer, a tree of high price and profit; also, diuers other fruit trees, some of them with strange barks, of an Orange colour, in feeling soft and smoothe like Veluet: in the thickest parts of these woods, you may see a furlong or more round about. On the Northwest side of this Iland, neere to the sea side, is a standing Lake of fresh water, almost three English miles in compasse, in the middest whereof stands a plot of woodie ground, an acre in quantitie or not aboue: this Lake is full of small Tortoises, and exceedingly frequented with all sorts of fowles before rehearsed, which breed, some lowe on the banks, and others on lowe trees about this Lake in great abundance, whose young ones of all sorts we tooke and eat at our pleasure; but all these fowles are much bigger than ours in England. Also, in euery Iland, and almost in euery part of euery Iland, are great store of Ground nuts, fortie together on a string, some of them as bigge as hennes egges; they grow not two inches vnder ground: the which nuts we found to be as good as Potatoes. Also, diuers sorts of shell-fish, as Scallops, Muscles, Cockles, Lobsters, Crabs, Oisters, and Wilks, exceeding good and very great. But not to cloy you with particular rehearsall of such things as God & Nature hath bestowed on these places, in comparison wherof, the most fertil part of al England is (of it selfe) but barren; we went in our light-horsman frō this Iland to the maine, right against this Iland some two leagues off, where comming ashore, we stood a while like men rauished at the

Oakes. Cedars. Beech. Elme. Hollie. Walnut trees. Cherry trees.

Sassafras trees. Diuers other trees.

A lake three miles about.

Small Tortoises.

Abundance of fowles, much bigger than ours in England.

Ground nuts.

Shellfish.

The exceeding beautie of the maine land. Great Lakes. Large medowes.

beautie and delicacie of this sweet soile; for besides diuers cleere Lakes of fresh water (whereof we saw no end) Medowes very large and full of greene grasse; euen the most woody places (I speake onely of such as I saw) doe grow so distinct and apart, one tree from another, upon greene grassie ground, somewhat higher than the Plaines, as if Nature would shew herselfe aboue her power, artificiall. Hard by, we espied seuen Indians; and comming up to them, at first they expressed some feare; but being emboldned by our courteous usage, and some trifles which we gaue them, they followed us to a necke of land, which we imagined had beene seuered from the maine; but finding it otherwise, we perceiued a broad harbour or riuers mouth, which ranne up into the maine: but because the day was farre spent, we were forced to returne to the Island from whence we came, leauing the discouerie of this harbour, for a time of better leasure: of the goodnesse of which harbour, as also of many others thereabouts, there is small doubt, considering that all the Islands, as also the maine (where we were) is all rockie grounds and broken lands. Now the next day, we determined to fortifie our selues in the little plot of ground in the midst of the Lake aboue mentioned, where we built an house, and couered it with sedge, which grew about this lake in great abundance; in building whereof, we spent three weeks and more: but the second day after our comming from the maine, we espied 9 canowes or boats, with fiftie Indians in them, comming toward us from this part of the maine, where we, two daies before, landed; and being loth they should discouer our fortification, we went out on the sea side to meet them; and comming somewhat neere them, they all sat downe upon the stones, calling aloud to us (as we rightly ghessed) to doe the like, a little distance from them: hauing sat a while in this order, captaine Gosnold willed me to go unto them, to see what countenance they would make; but assone as I came up unto them, one of them, to whom I had giuen a knife two daies before in the maine, knew me (whom I also very wel remembred) and smiling upon me, spake somewhat unto their lord or captaine, which sat in the midst of them, who presently rose up and tooke a large Beauer skin from one that stood about

Seuen Indians.

A broad riuer.

A good harbour.

The English house.

Nine canoas with fiftie Indians in them.

Their captaine.

him

him, and gaue it vnto me, which I requited for that time the best I could: but I pointing towards captaine Gosnold, made signes vnto him, that he was our captaine, and desirous to be his friend, and enter league with him, which (as I perceiued) he vnderstood, and made signes of ioy: whereupon captaine Gosnold with the rest of his companie, being twentie in all, came vp vnto them; and after many signes of gratulations (captaine Gosnold presenting their L. with certeine trifles which they wondred at, and highly esteemed) we became very great friends, and sent for meat aboord our shallop, and gaue them such meats as we had then readie dressed, whereof they misliked nothing but our mustard, whereat they made many a sowre face. While we were thus merry, one of them had conueied a target of ours into one of their canowes, which we suffered, onely to trie whether they were in subiection to this L. to whom we made signes (by shewing him another of the same likenesse, and pointing to the canowe) what one of his companie had done: who suddenly expressed some feare, and speaking angerly to one about him (as we perceiued by his countenance) caused it presently to be brought backe againe. So the rest of the day we spent in trading with them for Furres, which are Beauers, Luzernes, Marterns, Otters, Wild-cat skinnes very large and deepe Furre, blacke Foxes, Conie skinnes, of the colour of our Hares, but somewhat lesse, Deere skinnes very large, Seale skinnes, and other beasts skinnes, to vs vnknowen. They haue also great store of Copper, some very redde, and some of a paler colour; none of them but haue chaines, earrings or collars of this mettall: they head some of their arrows herewith, much like our broad arrow heads, very workmanly made. Their chaines are many hollow pieces semented together, ech piece of the bignesse of one of our reeds, a finger in length, ten or twelue of them together on a string, which they weare about their necks: their collars they weare about their bodies like bandelieres a handfull broad, all hollow pieces, like the other, but somewhat shorter, foure hundred pieces in a collar, very fine and euenly set together. Besides these, they haue large drinking cups, made like sculles, and other thinne plates of Copper, made much

Seuerall sorts of Furres.

Red Copper in abundance.

Chaines.

Collars.

Drinking cuppes of Copper.

much like our boare-speare blades, all which they so little esteeme, as they offered their fairest collars or chaines, for a knife or such like trifle, but we seemed little to regard it; yet I was desirous to understand where they had such store of this mettall, and made signes to one of them (with whom I was verie familiar) who taking a piece of Copper in his hand, made a hole with his finger in the ground, and withall, pointed to the maine from whence they came. They strike fire in this maner; euery one carrieth about him in a purse of tewed leather, a Minerall stone (which I take to be their Copper) and with a flat Emerie stone (wherewith Glasiers cut glasse, and Cutlers glase blades) tied fast to the end of a little sticke, gently he striketh upon the Minerall stone, and within a stroke or two, a sparke falleth upon a piece of Touchwood (much like our Spunge in England) and with the least sparke he maketh a fire presently. We had also of their Flaxe, wherewith they make many strings and cords, but it is not so bright of colour as ours in England: I am perswaded they haue great store growing upon the maine, as also Mines and many other rich commodities, which we, wanting both time and meanes, could not possibly discouer. Thus they continued with us three daies, euery night retiring themselues to the furthermost part of our Iland two or three miles from our fort: but the fourth day they returned to the maine, pointing fiue or six times to the Sun, and once to the maine, which we understood, that within fiue or six daies they would come from the maine to us againe: but being in their canowes a little from the shore, they made huge cries & shouts of ioy unto us; and we with our trumpet and cornet, and casting up our cappes into the aire, made them the best farewell we could: yet six or seuen of them remained with us behinde, bearing us company euery day into the woods, and helpt us to cut and carie our Sassafras, and some of them lay aboord our ship. These people, as they are exceeding courteous, gentle of disposition, and well conditioned, excelling all others that we haue seene; so for shape of bodie and louely fauour, I thinke they excell all the people of America; of stature much higher than we; of complexion or colour, much like a darke Oliue; their eie-browes and haire blacke, which they weare

Mines of Copper.

Minerall stones, Emerie stones.

Flaxe.

Indians apt for seruice.

Sassafras.

A goodly people, & of good conditions.

weare long, tied vp behinde in knots, whereon they pricke feathers of fowles, in fashion of a crownet: some of them are blacke thin bearded; they make beards of the haire of beasts: and one of them offered a beard of their making to one of our sailers, for his that grew on his face, which because it was of a red colour, they iudged to be none of his owne. They are quicke eied, and stedfast in their lookes, fearelesse of others harmes, as intending none themselues; some of the meaner sort giuen to filching, which the very name of Saluages (not weighing their ignorance in good or euill) may easily excuse: their garments are of Deere skins, and some of them weare Furres round and close about their necks. They pronounce our language with great facilitie; for one of them one day sitting by me, vpon occasion I spake smiling to him these words: How now (sirha) are you so saucie with my Tabacco? which words (without any further repetition) he suddenly spake so plaine and distinctly, as if he had beene a long scholar in the language. Many other such trials we had, which are heere needlesse to repeat. Their women (such as we saw) which were but three in all, were but lowe of stature, their eie-browes, haire, apparell, and maner of wearing, like to the men, fat, and very well fauoured, and much delighted in our companie; the men are very dutifull towards them. And truely, the holsomnesse and temperature of this Climat, doth not onely argue this people to be answerable to this description, but also of a perfect constitution of body, actiue, strong, healthfull, and very wittie, as the sundry toies of theirs cunningly wrought, may easily witnes. For the agreeing of this Climat with vs (I speake of my selfe, & so I may iustly do for the rest of our companie) that we found our health & strength all the while we remained there, so to renew and increase, as notwithstanding our diet and lodging was none of the best, yet not one of our company (God be thanked) felt the least grudging or inclination to any disease or sicknesse, but were much fatter and in better health than when we went out of England. But after our barke had taken in so much Sassafras, Cedar, Furres, Skinnes, and other commodities, as were thought conuenient; some of our company that had promised captaine Gosnold to stay, hauing nothing but a sa-

Their apparell.

Their women.

The goodnesse of the Climat.

uing voyage in their minds, made our company of inhabitants (which was small enough before) much smaller; so as captaine Gosnold seeing his whole strength to consist but of twelue men, and they but meanly prouided, determined to Their returne. returne for England, leauing this Island (which he called Elizabeths Island) with as many true sorrowfull eies, as were before desirous to see it. So the 18 of June, being Friday, we weighed, and with indifferent faire winde and weather came to anker the 23 of July, being also Friday (in all, bare fiue weeks) before Exmouth.

Your Lordships to command,
Iohn Brereton.

A briefe Note of such commodities as we saw *in the countrey notwithstanding our small* time of stay.

Trees.

SAssafras trees, the roots wherof at 3.s. the pound are 336.l. the tunne.
Cedars tall and straight, in great abundance.
Cypres trees.
Oakes.
Walnut trees great store.
Elmes.
Beech.
Hollie.
Hassenut trees.
Cherry trees.
Cotten trees.
Other fruit trees to vs vnknowen.

The finder of our Sassafras in these parts, was one Master Robert Meriton.

Fowles.

EAgles.
Hernshawes.
Cranes.
Bitters.
Mallards.
Teales.
Geese.
Pengwins.
Ospreis and Hawks.
Crowes.
Rauens.
Mewes.
Doues.
Sea-pies.
Blacke-birds with carnation wings.

Beasts.

DEere in great store, very great and large.
Beares.

Beares.
Luzernes.
Blacke Foxes.
Beavers.
Otters.
Wilde-Cats, verie large and great.
Dogs like Foxes, blacke and sharpe nosed.
Conies.

Fruits, Plants, and Herbs.

TAbacco, excellent sweet and strong.
Vines in more plenty than in *France*.
Ground-nuts, good meat, & also medicinable.
Strawberries.
Raspeberries.
Gooseberries.
Hurtleberries.
Pease growing naturally.
Flaxe.
Sorrell, & manie other herbs wherewith they made sallets.

Fishes.

WHales.
Tortoises, both on land and sea.
Seales.
Cods.
Mackerell.
Breames.
Herrings.
Thornbacke.
Hakes.
Rockefish.
Doggefish.
Lobsters.
Crabbes.
Muscles.
Wilks.
Cockles.
Scallops.
Oisters.

SNakes foure foot in length, and sixe inches about, which the Indians eat for daintie meat, the skinnes whereof they vse for girdles.

Mettals and Stones.

COpper in great abundance.
Emerie stones for Glasiers & Cutlers.
Alabaster very white.
Stones glistering and shining like Minerall stones,
Stones of a blue mettalline colour, which we take to be Steele oare.
Stones of all sorts for buildings.
Cley, red and white.

A briefe Note of the sending another barke *this present yeere 1602, by the honourable* knight, Sir WALTER RALEGH, for the searching out of his Colonie in *Virginia.*

SAmuel Mace of Weimouth, a very sufficient Mariner, an honest sober man, who had béene at Virginia twise before, was imploied thither by Sir Walter Ralegh, to finde those people which were left there in the yéere 1587. To whose succour he hath sent fiue seuerall times at his owne charges. The parties by him set forth, performed nothing; some of them following their owne profit elsewhere; others returning with friuolous allegations. At this last time, to auoid all excuse, he bought a barke, and hired all the company for wages by the moneth: who departing from Weimouth in March last 1602, fell fortie leagues to the Southwestward of Hatarask, in thirtie foure degrées or thereabout; and hauing there spent a moneth; when they came along the coast to séeke the people, they did it not, pretending that the extremitie of weather and losse of some principall ground-tackle, forced and feared them from searching the port of Hatarask, to which they were sent. From that place where they abode, they brought Sassafras, Radix Chinæ or the China root, Beniamin, Cassia lignea, & a rinde of a trée more strong than any spice as yet knowen, with diuers other commodities, which hereafter in a larger discourse may come to light.

A Treatise

A Treatise, conteining important inducements *for the planting in these parts, and finding a passage* that way to the South sea and *China*.

THe voiage which we intend, is to plant Christian people & religion vpon the Northwest countreis of America, in places temperat and well agreeing with our constitution, which though the same do lie betweene 40 & 44 degrees of latitude, vnder the Paralels of Italie & France, yet are not they so hot; by reason that the suns heat is qualified in his course ouer the Ocean, before he arriueth vpon the coasts of America, attracting much vapour from the sea: which mitigation of his heat, we take for a benefit to vs that intend to inhabit there; because vnder the Climat of 40 degrees, the same would be too vehement els for our bodies to endure. Temperate Climats.

These lands were neuer yet actually possessed by any Christian prince or people, yet often intended to be by the French nation, which long sithence had inhabited there, if domesticall warres had not withheld them: notwithstanding the same are the rightfull inheritance of her Maiestie, being first discouered by our nation in the time of King Henrie the seuenth, vnder the conduct of John Cabot and his sonnes: by which title of first discouery, the kings of Portugall and Spaine doe holde and enioy their ample and rich kingdomes in their Indies East and West; and also lately planted in part by the Colonies sent thither by the honourable knight, Sir Walter Ralegh. Her Maiesties title.

The course vnto these countreys, is thorow the Ocean, altogether free from all restraint by forren princes to be made; whereunto other our accustomed trades are subiect; apt for most winds that can blow, to be performed commonly in 30 A commodious and safe course.

or 35 daies. The coast faire, with safe roads and harbors for ships: Many riuers.

Riuers.

Fertile lands.

These lands be faire and pleasant, resembling France, intermedled with mountaines, valleys, medowes, woodlands, and champians. The soile is exceeding strong, by reason it was neuer manured; and will be therefore most fit to beare at first, Rape-seeds, Hempe, Flax, and whatsoeuer els requireth such strong soile. Rape-oiles, and all sorts of oiles, will be very commodious for England, which spendeth oiles abundantly about Clothing and Leather-dressing. In like sort, Hempe and Flax are profitable, whether the same be sent into England, or wrought there by our people; Oad also will grow there aswell or better then in Terçera.

Rape-oiles.

Dies.

The Saluages weare faire colours in some of their attire, whereby we hope to find rich dies and colours for painting.

The trees are for the most part, Cedars, Pines, Spruse, Firre, and Oaks to the Northward. Of these trees will be drawen Tarre and Pitch, Rosen, Turpentine, and Soape-ashes. They will make masts for the greatest shippes of the world. Excellent timbers of Cedar, and boords for curious buildings.

Minerals.

Copper.

The cliffes vpon the coasts and mountaines euery where shew great likelihood of Minerals. A very rich mine of Copper is found, whereof I haue seene proofe; and the place described. Not farre from which there is a great hope also of a Siluer mine. There be faire quarries of stone, of beautifull colours, for buldings.

Grapes.

The ground bringeth forth without industrie, Pease, Roses, Grapes, Hempe, besides other plants, fruits, herbs and flowers, whose pleasant view and delectable smelles, doe demonstrate sufficiently the fertilitie and sweetnesse of that soile and aire.

Beasts.

Beasts of many kindes; some of the bignesse of an Oxe, whose hides make good Buffe: Deere, both red and of other sorts in abundance: Luzerns, Marterns, Sables, Beauers, Beares, Otters, Wolues, Foxes, and Squirrels, which to the Northward are blacke, and accounted very rich Furres.

Fowles.

Fowles both of the water and land, infinit store and varietie; Hawks both short and long winged, Partridges in abundance,

bundance, which are very great, and easily taken. Birds great and small, some like unto our Blacke-birds, others like Canarie-birds: And many (aswell birds as other creatures) strange and differing from ours of Europe

Fish, namely, Cods, which as we encline more unto the South, are more large and vendible for England and France, than the Newland fish. Whales and Seales in great abundance. Oiles of them are rich commodities for England, whereof we now make Soape, besides many other uses. Item, Tunneys, Anchoues, Bonits, Salmons, Lobsters, Oisters hauing Pearle, and infinit other sorts of fish, which are more plentifull upon those Northwest coasts of America, than in any parts of the knowen world. Salt is reported to be found there, which els may be made there, to serue sufficiently for all fishing. Fish.

So as the commodities there to be raised both of the sea and land (after that we haue planted our people skilfull and industrious) will be, Fish, Whale and Seale oiles, Soape ashes and Soape, Tarre and Pitch, Rosen and Turpentine, Masts, Timber and boords of Cedars, Firres, and Pines, Hempe, Flaxe, Cables and Ropes, Saile-clothes, Grapes, and Raisens and Wines, Corne, Rape-seeds & oiles, Hides, Skinnes, Furres, Dies and Colours for painting, Pearle, Mettals, and other Minerals. Commodities in generall.

These commodities before rehearsed, albeit for the most part they be grosse, yet are the same profitable for the State of England specially, aswell in regard of the use of such commodities, as for the imploiment also of our people and ships; the want whereof, doth decay our townes and ports of England, and causeth the realme to swarme full with poore and idle people. Imploiment of our people, and repairing decaied ports.

These commodities in like sort, are of great use and estimation in all the South and Westerne countreys of Europe; namely, Italie, France and Spaine: for the which all nations that haue beene accustomed to repaire unto the Newfoundland for the commoditie of fish and oiles alone, will henceforward forsake the Newfound-land, and trade with us, when once we haue planted people in those parts: by whose industrie shall be prouided for all commers, both fish and oiles, The trade to Newfound-land shalbe remoued to us.

and many commodities besides, of good importance & value.

Spanish commodities.

Then will the Spaniards and Portugals bring unto us in exchange of such commodities before mentioned, Wines, Sweet oiles, Fruits, Spices, Sugars, Silks, Gold and Silver, or whatsoever that Europe yeeldeth, to supply our necessities, and to increase our delights.

English commodities.

For which Spanish commodities and other sorts likewise, our merchants of England will bring unto us againe, Cloth, Cattell, for our store and breed; and every thing els that we shall need, or that England shall haply exchange for such commodities.

Vent of our Cloth.

By this intercourse, our habitations will be made a Staple of all vendible commodities of the world, and a meanes to vent a very great quantitie of our English cloth into all the cold regions of America extended very farre.

Intercourse will soone be had with other nacions.

This intercourse also wil be soone drawen together by this reason: That neere adioining upon the same coasts of Newfound-land, is the greatest fishing of the world; whither doe yeerely repaire about 400 sailes of ships, for no other commoditie than Fish and Whale-oiles. Then forasmuch as merchants are diligent inquisitours after gaines, they will soone remoove their trade from Newfound-land unto us neere at hand, for so great increase of gaine as they shall make by trading with us. For whereas the voyage unto the Newfound-land is into a more cold and intemperate place, not to be traded nor frequented at all times, not fortified for securitie of the ships and goods, oft spoiled by pirats or men of warre; the charges great for salt; double manning and double victualling their ships, in regard that the labor is great and the time long, before their lading can be made readie: they cary outwards no commodities nor fraight; and after sixe moneths voyage, their returne is made but of Fish and Oiles.

Incommodities in the Newland trade.

Commodities by having trade with us.

Contrariwise, by trading with us at our intended place, the course shalbe in a maner as short; into a more temperate and healthfull climat; at all times of the yeere to be traded; harbors fortified to secure ships and goods; charges abridged of salt, victualling and manning ships double: because lading shall be provided unto their hands at a more easie rate than themselves could make it. They shall carry fraight also out-

ward

ward, to make exchange with vs; and so get profit both waies: and then euery foure moneths they may make a voyage and returne, of both fish and oiles, and many other commodities of good worth.

These reasons aduisedly weighed, shall make our enterprise appeare easie, and the most profitable of the world, for our nation to vndertake. The reasons we chiefly relie vpon, are these: namely, *Note.*

1 Those lands which we intend to inhabit, shall minister vnto our people, the subiect and matter of many notable commodities.

2 England shall affoord vs people both men, women and children aboue 10000, which may very happily be spared from hence to work those commodities there.

3 Newfound-land shall minister shipping to carrie away all our commodities, and to bring others vnto vs againe for our supplie.

Now two of these reasons are already effected vnto our hands: that is to say: The place where we shall finde rich commodities, and ships to vent them. It remaineth onely for our parts, to carrie and transport people with their prouisions from England, where the miserie and necessitie of manie crie out for such helpe and reliefe. *An easie enterprise, and great reward.*

This considered, no nation of Christendom is so fit for this action as England, by reason of our superfluous people (as I may tearme them) and of our long domesticall peace. And after that we be once 200 men strong, victualled and fortified, we can not be remoued by as many thousands. *The English nation most fit for discoueries.*

For besides that, we haue seene both in France and the Low-countreys, where 200 men well fortified and victualled, haue kept out the forces both of the French & Spanish kings, euen within their owne kingdomes: it shalbe also a matter of great difficulty, to transport an army ouer the Ocean with victuals and munition, and afterwards to abide long siege abroad, against vs fortified within, where the very elements and famine shall fight for vs, though we should lie still and defend onely.

The Saluages vnable to defend or offend.

The Saluages neither in this attempt shall hurt vs, they being simple, naked and vnarmed, destitute of edge-tooles or weapons; wherby they are vnable either to defend thẽselues or to offend vs: neither is our intent to prouoke, but to cherish and win them vnto Christianitie by faire meanes; yet not to trust them too far, but to prouide against all accidents.

Then to conclude, as we of all other nations are most fit for a discouery and planting in remote places; euen so, vnder the heauens there is no place to be found so conuenient for such a purpose; by reason of the temperature, commodities, apt site for trade, & repaire thither already of so many ships, which in any other vnfrequented countrey, can not be procured in a mans age, nor with expense of halfe a million.

This action but set on foot, will goe forward of it selfe.

So as the onely difficultie now, is in our first preparation to transport some few people at the beginning; the charges whereof shall be defraied by our first returne of fish and some commodities of Sassafras, Hides, Skinnes and Furres, which we shall also haue by trading with the Saluages. The profe of which commodities shall incourage our merchants to venter largely in the next. The supplie shall easily and continually be sent by ships, which yeerely goe from hence vnto the Newfound-land and vs; and the intercourse & exchange we shall haue with all nations repairing thither, shall store vs with abundance of all things for our necessities and delights. Which reasons, if they had beene foreseene of them that planted in the South part of Virginia (which is a place destitute of good harbours, and farre from all trade) no doubt but if they had setled neerer vnto this frequented trade in the Newfound-land, they had by this time beene a very flourishing State, and plentifull in all things; who also might then haue made way into the bowels of that large continent, where assuredly we shall discouer verie goodly and rich kingdomes and cities.

Ouersight in choise of a new habitation.

A matter of importance for England.

It may also seeme a matter of great consequence for the good and securitie of England; that out of these Northerly regions we shall be able to furnish this realme of all maner of prouisions for our nauies; namely, Pitch, Rosen, Cables, Ropes, Masts, and such like; which shall be made within those her Maiesties owne dominions, by her owne subiects,

and

and brought hither thorow the Ocean, free from restraint of any other prince; whereby the customes and charges bestowed by our merchants (to the inriching of forren Estates) shalbe lessened, and turned to the benefit of her Highnesse and her deputies in those parts: which also shall deliuer our merchants from many troubles & molestations which they now vnwillingly indure in our East trades; and shal make vs the lesse to doubt the malice of those States whom now we may not offend, lest we should be intercepted of the same prouisions, to the weakening of our nauie, the most roiall defence of this noble realme.

Of a conuenient passage and trade into the South Sea, vnder temperate regions, part by riuers, and some part ouer land, in the continent of *America*.

I Will adde héereunto an assured hope (grounded vpon infallible reasons) of a way to be made, part ouer land, & part by riuers or lakes, into the South seas vnto Cathay, China, and those passing rich countreys, lying in the East parts of the world: which way or passage (supposed to be beyond the vttermost bounds of America, vnder the frozen Zone) is neuerthelesse, held by the opinion of many learned writers and men of iudgement now liuing, to be in these more temperate regions; and that the same shall neuer be made knowen, vnlesse we plant first; whereby we shall learne as much by inquisition of the naturall inhabitants, as by our owne nauigations. I will not héerein relie vpon reports made in the French mens discoueries; that the sea which giueth passage vnto Cathay, extendeth from the North, néere vnto the riuer of Canada, into 44 degrées, where the same of the Saluages is called Tadouac.

Neither vpon the discoueries of Iaques Noel, who hauing passed beyond the thrée Saults, where Iaques Cartier left to discouer, finding the riuer of S. Laurence passable on the other side or branch; and afterwards, vnderstood of the inhabitants that the same riuer did leade into a mightie lake, which at the entrance was fresh, but beyond, was bitter or salt; the end whereof was vnknowen.

Omitting therefore these hopes, I will ground my opinion vpon reason and nature, which will not faile.

For this we know alreadie, that great riuers haue béene discouered a thousand English miles into that continent of America; namely, that of S. Laurence or Canada. But not regarding miles more or lesse, most assuredly, that and other knowen riuers there, doe descend from the highest parts or mountaines, or middle of that continent, into our North sea. And like as those mountains do cast from them, streames into our North seas; euen so the like they do into the South sea, which is on the backe of that continent.

A large course of a riuer thorow a mightie continent, produceth a portable riuer.

For all mountaines haue their descents toward the seas about them, which are the lowest places and proper mansions of water: and waters (which are conteined in the mountaines, as it were in cisternes) descending naturally, doe alwaies resort vnto the seas inuironing those lands: for example; From the Alps confining Germanie, France, and Italie, the mightie riuer Danubie doth take his course East, and dischargeth into the Pontique sea: the Rhine, North, and falleth into the Germane sea: the Rhosne, West, and goeth into the Mediterran sea: the Po, South, is emptied into the Adriatick or gulfe of Venice. Other instances may be produced to like effect in Africk; yea, at home amongst the mountaines in England.

Séeing then in nature this can not be denied, and by experience elsewhere is found to be so, I will shew how a trade may be disposed more commodiously into the South sea thorow these temperate and habitable regions, than by the frozen Zones in the supposed passages of Northwest or Northeast: where, if the very moment be omitted of the time to passe, then are we like to be frozen in the seas, or forced to Winter in extreame colde and darkenesse like vnto hell: or in the midst of Summer, we shalbe in perill to haue our ships ouerwhelmed or crusht in pieces by hideous and fearefull mountaines of yce floting vpon those seas.

Therefore foure Staple-places must be erected, when the most short and passable way is found: that is to say, two

vpon

vpon the North side, at the head and fal of the riuer; and two others on the South side, at the head and fal also of that other riuer.

Prouided, that ships may passe vp those riuers vnto the Staples, so farre as the same be nauigable into the land; and afterwards, that boats with flat bottomes may also passe so high and neere the heads of the riuers vnto the Staples, as possibly they can, euen with lesse than two foot water, which can not then be far from the heads; as in the riuer of Chagre.

That necke or space of land betweene the two heads of the said riuers, if it be 100 leagues (which is not like) the commodities from the North and from the South sea brought thither, may wel be carried ouer the same vpon horses, mules or beasts of that countrey apt to labour (as the elke or buffel) or by the aid of many Saluages accustomed to burdens; who shall stead vs greatly in these affaires.

It is moreouer to be considered, that all these countreys do yeeld (so farre as is knowen) Cedars, Pines, Firre trees and Oaks, to build, mast, and yeard ships; wherefore we may not doubt, but that ships may be builded on the South sea.

Then as ships on the South side may goe and returne to and from Cathay, China, and other most rich regions of the East world in fiue moneths or thereabouts; euen so the goods being carried ouer vnto the North side, ships may come thither from England to fetch the same goods, and returne by a voyage of foure or fiue moneths vsually.

So as in euery foure moneths may be returned into England the great riches of Cathay, China, Iapan, and the rest, which will be Spices, Drugges, Muske, Pearle, Stones, Gold, Siluer, Silks, Clothes of gold, & all maner of precious things, which shall recompense the time and labour of their transportation and carriage, if it were as farre and dangerous as the Mores trade is from Fess and Marocco (ouer the burning and moueable sands, in which they perish many times, and suffer commonly great distresses) vnto the riuer called Niger in Africa, and from thence, vp the said riuer manie hundred miles; afterwards ouer-land againe, vnto the riuer Nilus; and so vnto Cairo in Egypt, from whence they returne the way they came.

Or if it were a voyage so farre as our merchants haue made into Persia, euen to Ormus, by the way of the North, through Rusia into the Caspian sea, and so forth, with paiment of many tolles. But this passage ouer and thorow the continent of America, as the same shall be alwaies vnder temperate and habitable climats; and a pleasant passage, after it hath béene a little frequented; euen so it must fall out much shorter than it séemeth, by false description of that continent, which doth not extend so farre into the West, as by later nauigations is found and described in more exquisit charts. Besides that, the sea extends it selfe into the land very farre in many places on the South side; whereby our accesse vnto the South ocean, shall be by so much, the shorter.

FINIS.

CPSIA information can be obtained
at www.ICGtesting.com
Printed in the USA
BVHW061620031218
534640BV00035B/2967/P

9 781528 326063